I0407886

Mandala
Miracle Coloring Art

Copyright: Published in the United States by Karen Sanderson
Published January 2017
ISBN-13: 978-1542679640
ISBN-10: 1542679648

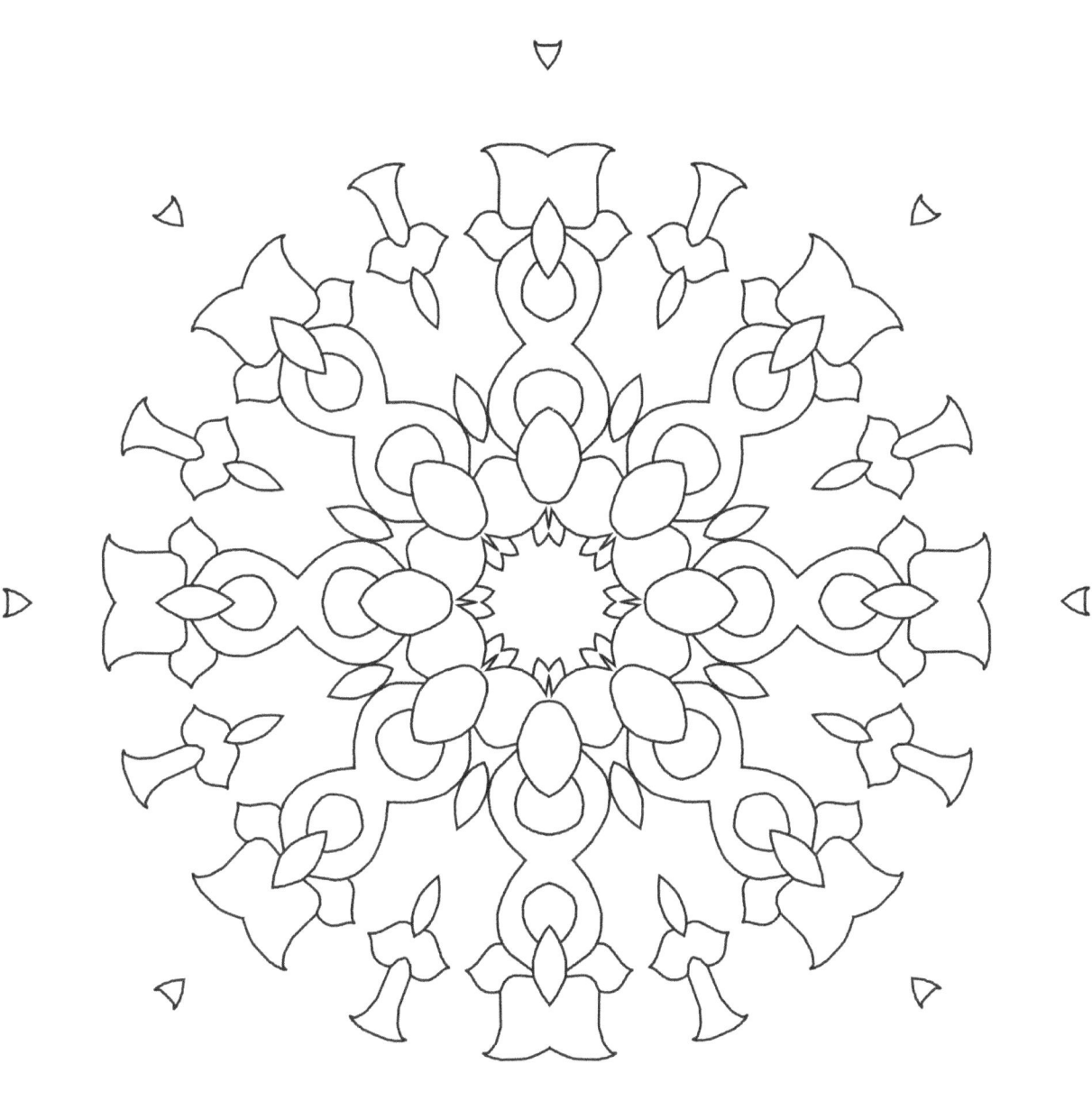

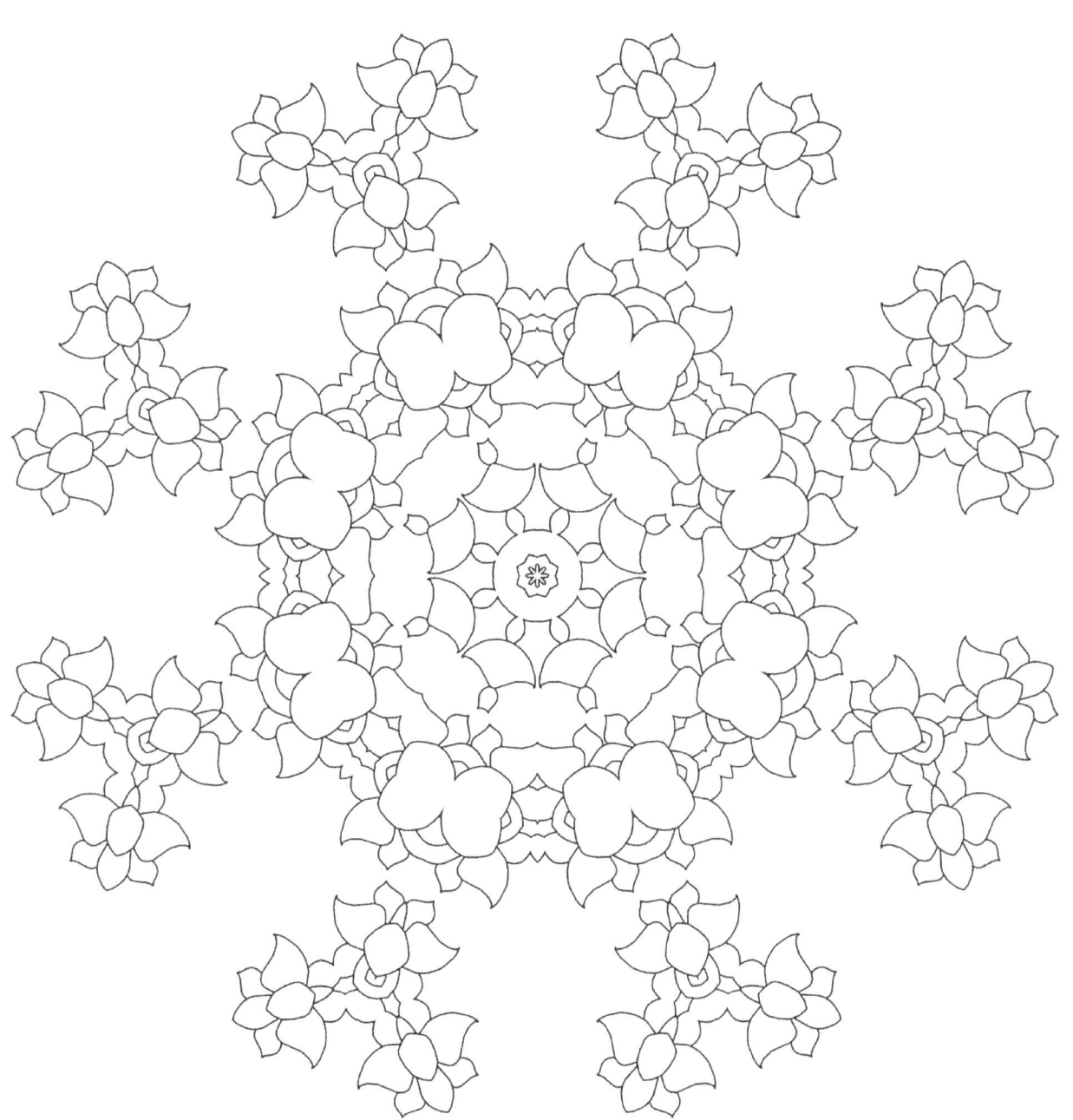

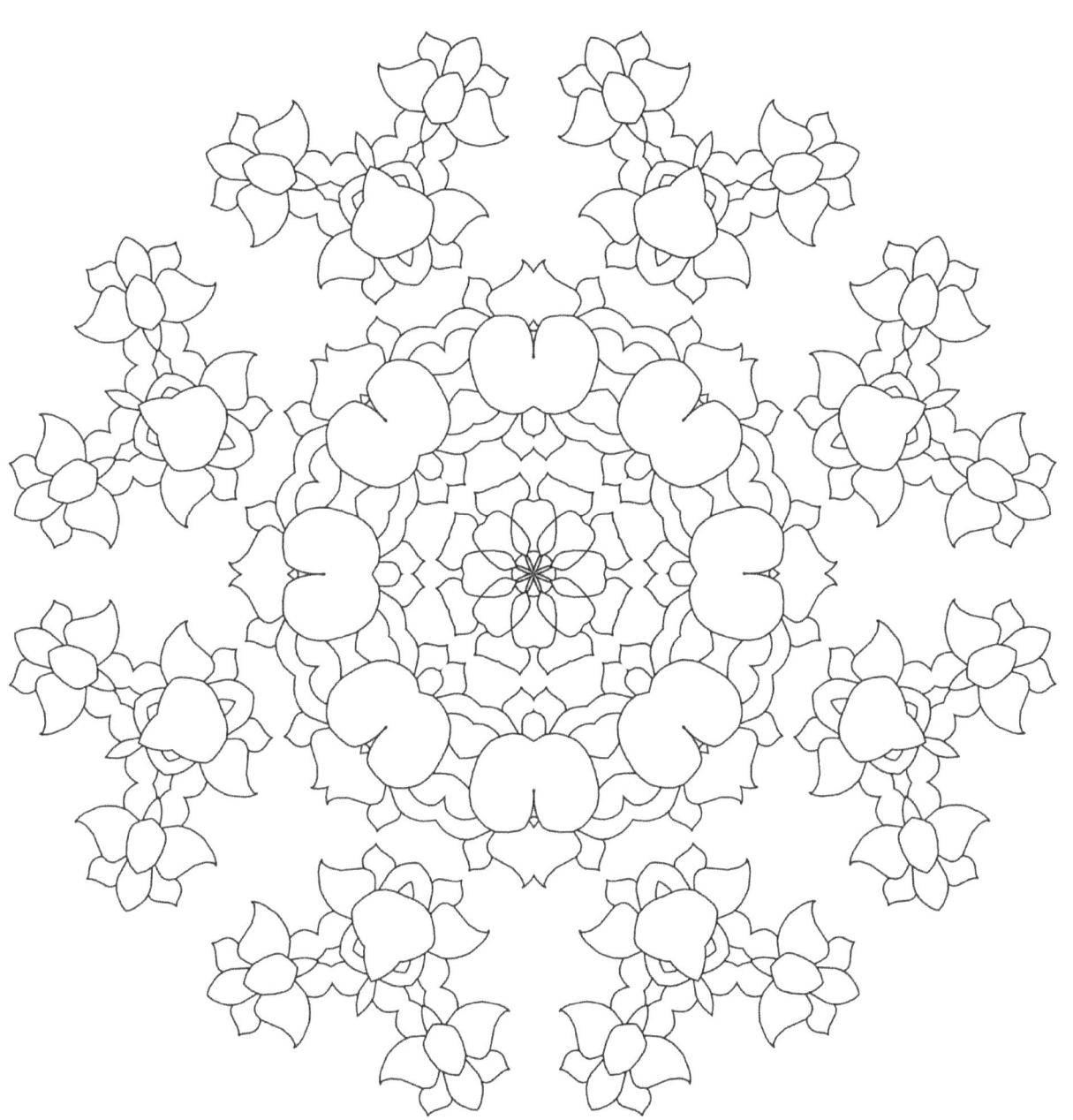

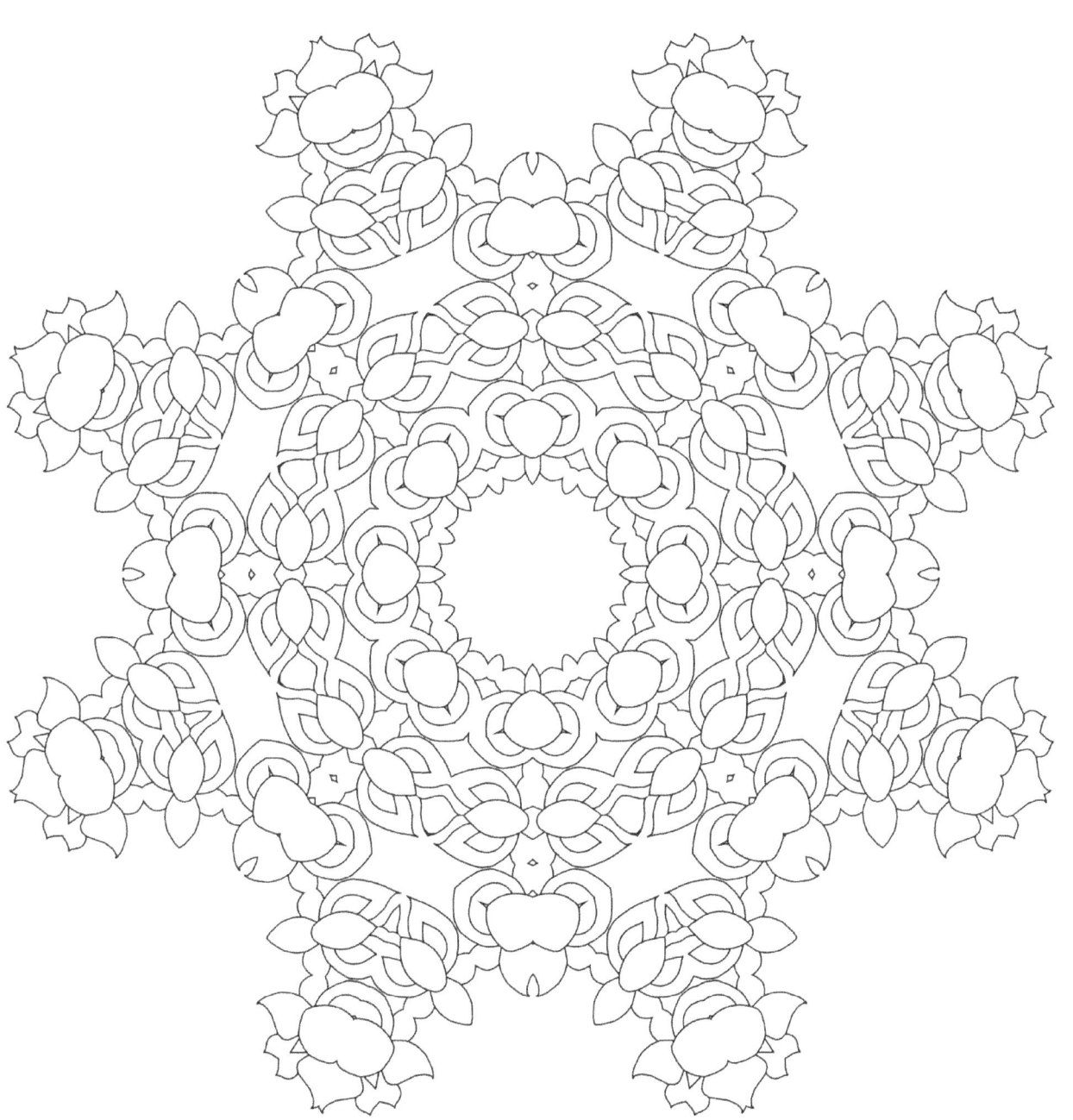

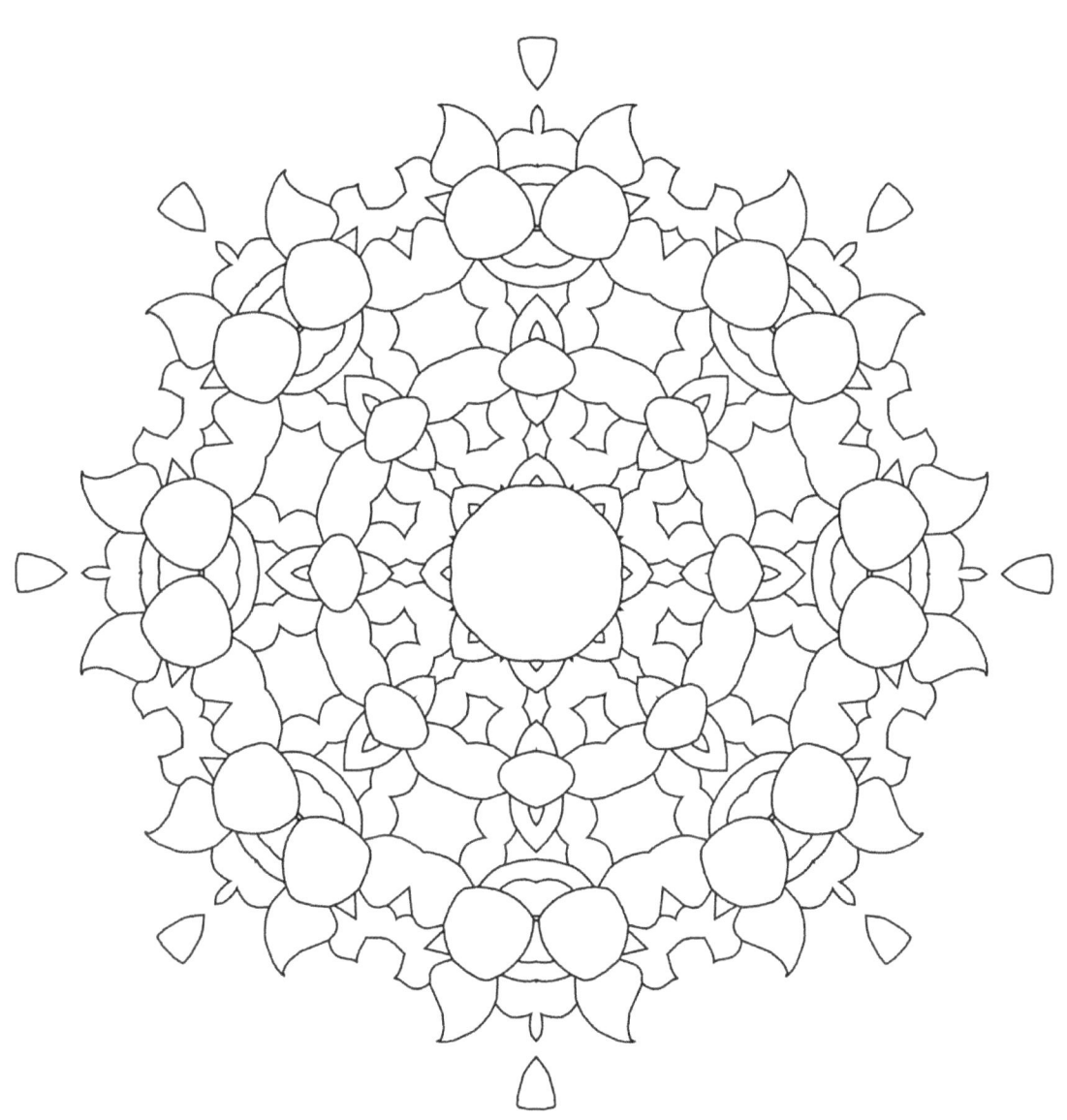

Thank you

www.ingramcontent.com/pod-product-compliance
Lightning Source LLC
Chambersburg PA
CBHW081555280526
45788CB00011B/3481